I0458608

Bookworm 101

A Guide for Book Reviewers and Bookish Content Creators

First Edition

***

by R.L. Zareva

***

Compendia Publishing, 2025.

Copyright © 2025 by Compendia Publishing. All rights reserved.

No part of this publication may be reproduced, stored in a retrieval system, or transmitted in any form by any means, electronic, mechanical, photocopying, recording, or otherwise, without the prior written permission of the copyright owner.

No part of this publication may be used to develop and/or train artificial intelligence models, systems, or technology, with no exception for any AI-related uses that fall under the category of fair use or general-purpose AI. No part of this publication that has been made publicly available online may be used in general web scraping, text or data mining practices, and/or any AI-related transformative uses.

First published in the digital version with ISBN: 978-1-963038-37-8, January 1st '2025.

Paperback print ISBN: 978-1-963038-82-8, published on June 13th '2025.

The neurodivergent version paperback print ISBN: 978-1-963038-33-0.

Cover photo: Strahov Library, Prague, Czech Republic, by Tilia Lucida.

***

Library of Congress Control Number: 2025930737

Published by Compendia Publishing, Wilmington, DE, USA.

https://www.compendiapublishing.com

Contents

Fair Warning

This book contains subjects related to geopolitical differences and anthropological perspectives. It is not suitable for readers with sensitivity to certain subjects and/or language expressions. Readers' discretion is advised.

This publication is NOT suitable for minors. The age of majority may vary from one area of jurisdiction to another. In the absence of clear guidance and/or limitations from the governing bodies, the publisher and author suggest that 18 years of age be the minimum age for reading this publication.

Disclaimer

The publisher and author support the continuation of education and learning. This publication may be included as a subject to study and criticise in the language arts, literature, culture, business, creator economy, or any other related department or faculty.

The manuscript and cover of this publication are not generated by any artificial intelligence system. No part of this publication may be used to develop and/or train artificial intelligence models, systems, or technology, with no exception for any AI-related uses that fall under the category of fair use or general-purpose AI. No part of this publication that has been made publicly available online may be used in general web scraping, text or data mining practices, and/or any AI-related transformative uses.

Dedication

To my readers.
I don't care when you will read or review any of my published books. When someone squeezes my book in between the tight schedules, it already means a lot to me.

***

To content creators who have been shouting me out through the internet. Thank you for giving a chance to an author who came from some other side of the earth.

***

To all aspiring writers who started by reading books:
Keep staining those pages in front of you with ink (or carbon, whichever you would prefer).
When you hit the border, cross it!
Flip the page and do it again.

Reader's Journal by R. L. Zareva

Reader's Journal is the hardback version of the book "Bookworm 101: A Guide for Book Reviewers and Bookish Content Creators," completed with blank-dated planners, checklists, and trackers.

Morana and the Dragon Version ISBN: 978-1-963038-16-3

Lilith Version ISBN: 978-1-963038-20-0

Lilith in the Forest Version ISBN: 978-1-963038-21-7

Angel Statues Version ISBN: 978-1-963038-18-7

Falling Angel Version ISBN: 978-1-963038-25-5

Also by R. L. Zareva

Novels by Rada Lyubomirova

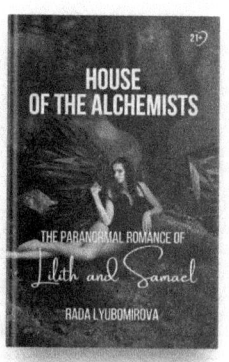

Novellas by Rada Lyubomirova

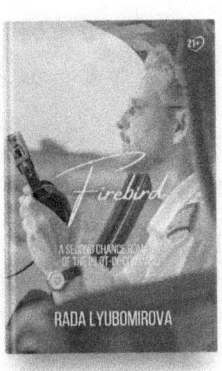 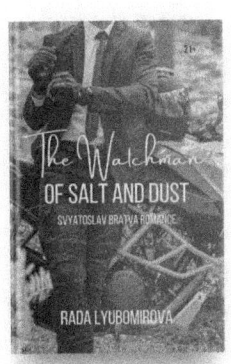

 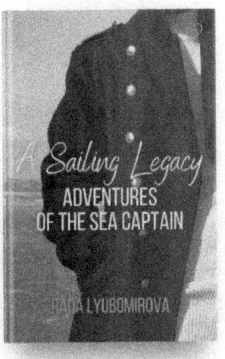

1

Instructions for Use

Whether you are reading the digital version or utilising the journal version of this book, I shall not leave you alone and confused as book reviewers.

The bookish content creators whose paths cross with mine on social media are wonderful people, regardless of whether or not they like my book.

Probably not many of my readers know that technical writing, building industry manuals, and user guides are some parts of what I do for my main job—of course they are filled with hyphenations, en dashes, and em dashes.

They have mostly never been published to the general public. Either they are classified, conducted under confidentiality requirements, or included in non-disclosure agreements (NDA), so that you may not be able to find them. They are to serve different purposes than the general public may need.

Before we start this guided journal, I need to admit that the intention of publishing it was to write a user guide or customer guide for readers in general. Readers of the digital version and the paperback print can have examples for building a customised journal according to one's needs.

Here I shall give you a glimpse into my work as a crew member in my industry. Here and now, you might be readers. Tomorrow you might be book reviewers making user-generated content.

Then you will be journalists undergoing editorial reviews or researchers doing peer reviews. One day you might also be an author, getting your own book published.

My genuine hope for your professional growth will be endless. Consider this user guide as your acquaintance to walk beside you along the journey.

Another thing to disclose is that R. L. Zareva is my pen name for nonfiction publications and technical writings. Even at the time this book manuscript is finalised, I have not told any of my family members that I write adult fiction under the pen name Rada Lyubomirova.

Some parts of my literary arts may (or may not) be considered unacceptable in the place I came from. That is the main reason for my faceless social media. It is not merely because I am not keen on giving any author's transparency.

Please be mindful that not every portion of land is a land of free speech. My publisher's team has been retaining my incognita left and right since deciding to publish my debut novel. Readers' understanding and consideration will be much appreciated.

2

To Be Read List

to Set Up the Budgets and Priorities

The TBR list is not always about the book we want to read. It can also be used as a personal tool for budgeting.

In the hardback journal version, journalers have the space to include 100 books. Each item on the list has a long underline to write down the book title and the author's name. These two are what we commonly put on our TBR list.

With how much social media has grown these days, it is very likely that we keep adding more and more books. There is nothing wrong with adding more to the list. I, too, am guilty of that.

When the reader has a medium-to-big account on social media, that might not be a problem. It is a common practice for authors and publishers to send books or promotional packages to bookish creators.

The issue comes when the reader is only starting out a social media account with a limited budget. The issue gets bigger if the creator lives in an area of jurisdiction that needs an expensive shipping cost.

The amount of cost might be doubled or tripled if the governing body applies tariffs on imported goods. To avoid wordy sentences, from this point of the user guide, the term "area(s) of jurisdiction" will be referred to as "region(s)."

The libraries' purchases might get cleared easier in the border crossing process than others. They are commonly considered public-benefit organisations.

All of my print books are in wide distribution worldwide. For every retailer and distributor, the publisher set the wholesale discount at 55% (at least for now, that is the rate). Hopefully it will give them leeway to set a discounted price for readers.

Can anyone imagine how upset we were when we found out that my books were highly marked up in Down Under? Even with that big portion of wholesale discount, they were still being marked up?

Unfortunately, yes. The publisher and I are still finding solutions for the matter. Please bear with us in the meantime. Our intention has never been to set the retail price high.

The discount is solely to compensate the retailers' effort in the customs clearance process. With their business tax identification number, hopefully, more books can cross the border faster. Even with that, sometimes it is not as easy as we hope it to be.

There is no signed copy of my books because I have not had the liberty to sign and send them. The rerouting process might cost the readers more time.

I, the author of my books, did order the print copies in May 2024, but even when this manuscript is finalised, this very author is still waiting for them to arrive.

Anyone who sees that some of my fiction works are only available in digital versions, please know that I have not put my hands on the print copies of them yet. It is not that I do not want to publish all of my books in print.

One day you may come across books by other authors that are available only in a digital version or vice versa. Please know that there are many factors to consider in publishing houses. Not all of our challenges are posted on social media.

The print version of this book is a different case. From more than a decade in technical writing, I have learnt how to delegate the quality assurance process. This user guide is nonfiction; fiction work, on the other hand, is a different beast.

***

It is time for us to continue on the TBR list. When you see the smaller boxes, they are to help you make priorities. If you have a sufficient budget, put a check mark on the box in front of the words "to buy". The alternative is to find out if your local library carries that book.

Libraries were also the pillars in the place I came from. Readers should not feel any shame in using those library cards. At least, that is my opinion.

Simply make a book request to the librarians for them to order the book. It is not only helping you but also helping other budgeted readers as well.

The publisher and I would appreciate readers who use the library cards rather than find anyone allegedly trying to pirate any book. That is one of the reasons why we keep rolling out eBook licences to give away.

Readers can get the licences to access our books by scanning or tapping the QR code we provide below. There is no sign-up or application needed to get the licences; they are for you to read.

Once you finish reading the book, the big boxes are for you to put a check mark on. To the next book to read, you go.

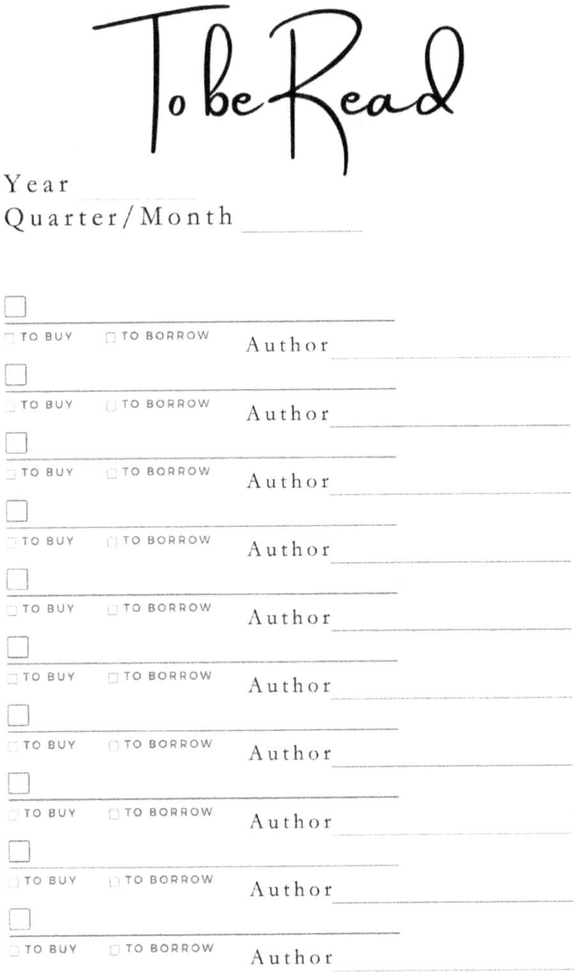

To be Read

Year _____
Quarter/Month _____

☐ _____
☐ TO BUY   ☐ TO BORROW   Author _____

☐ _____
☐ TO BUY   ☐ TO BORROW   Author _____

☐ _____
☐ TO BUY   ☐ TO BORROW   Author _____

☐ _____
☐ TO BUY   ☐ TO BORROW   Author _____

☐ _____
☐ TO BUY   ☐ TO BORROW   Author _____

☐ _____
☐ TO BUY   ☐ TO BORROW   Author _____

☐ _____
☐ TO BUY   ☐ TO BORROW   Author _____

☐ _____
☐ TO BUY   ☐ TO BORROW   Author _____

☐ _____
☐ TO BUY   ☐ TO BORROW   Author _____

☐ _____
☐ TO BUY   ☐ TO BORROW   Author _____

Image 2.1. TBR List Template

GOAL: MONTH:

PROGRESS TRACKER

0   5   10   15   20   25   30

PURPOSE OF THIS TRACKER
- [ ] READING
- [ ] REVIEW
- [ ] HABIT

Image 2.2. Tracker Template

Stationary
AND
SUPPLIES

☐
_____ ☐ TO BUY   ☐ IN STOCK
☐
_____ ☐ TO BUY   ☐ IN STOCK
☐
_____ ☐ TO BUY   ☐ IN STOCK
☐
_____ ☐ TO BUY   ☐ IN STOCK
☐
_____ ☐ TO BUY   ☐ IN STOCK
☐
_____ ☐ TO BUY   ☐ IN STOCK
☐
_____ ☐ TO BUY   ☐ IN STOCK
☐
_____ ☐ TO BUY   ☐ IN STOCK

Image 2.3. Stationary List Template

3

The Warnings

in the Front Matter

Book banning and/or censorship are not something unfamiliar to us. At least, in the place I came from, we grew up with this kind of norm.

There is the "18+" sign on this book cover. If my pen name, "Rada Lyubomirova", were never mentioned in this book, we could have put "14+" on it.

The governing bodies set the rules differently from one region to another. It is either 9, 15, 16, 17, 18, 19, 20, or even 21 years old. Because of that, the publisher and I refer to the highest one for the cover of my adult fiction works.

Regardless of how morally grey characters are depicted in my books, we know that it is the right thing to put "21+" on the cover. Consider it as our moral compass is calibrated prior to publication.

No, the sign on the top corner of the cover was never intended for the readers. Not everything that is shown means what it seems to be.

It may be considered small, but that is a part of the technical writing to guide the librarians and bookshop staff. We are to prevent my books from being placed in the wrong section of the library and bookshop.

If you find those signs helpful when deciding whether or not my books are suitable for your age, that will be something fulfilling for the publisher and me.

*****

Yet there is a relatively new discourse about "Trigger Warning" or "content warning".

So far, we have not found many books published by traditional publishing companies that carry on these warnings. Presumably, this is an indie or self-publishing thing.

The discourse that has been in circulation is either that the warning list is too much like the restaurant menu, vanishing the element of surprise in the story, or the warning list gets criticised because not every triggering element that each and every reader has is listed, like the restaurant menu.

Regardless of which is which, we might as well break them down. As for my books, here is the template of "Fair Warning" in the front matter. The explanations are numbered in relation to the superscripted numbers.

"This publication contains _____, _____, and _____. It is not suitable for readers with sensitivity to certain subjects and/or language expressions. Readers' discretion is advised.[1] This work of fiction is NOT suitable for minors. The age of majority may vary from one area of jurisdiction to another. In the absence of clear guidance and/or limitations from the governing bodies, the publisher and author suggest that 21 years of age be the minimum age for reading this publication."[2]

The fair warning above is intended for the governing bodies (or authorities) where the reader is located. The wording is standard, generic, and obviously does not look like a restaurant menu.

1. This advisory is to satisfy the requirement for entertaining materials in certain regions. There are still censorship committees (or agencies) in other parts of the world. As surreal as it sounds in this modern day and age, not in every portion of land, the freedom of speech is protected.

2. In the region where the age of majority is ruled lower than what we suggested, the reader who is no longer considered a minor by the governing bodies (or authorities) surely can read any of my books. Even if my fiction works are adult fiction filled with explicit romantic scenes, the reader can. It is neither my nor the publisher's place to judge anyone as being too young to read something or not, as long as the reader is in compliance with the limitation(s) being enforced in the said region.

***

The "Disclaimer" in the front matter of my books is never intended for the readers but for other related parties. Below is the template for my fiction writings:

"This publication is a work of fiction that draws inspiration from _____, with some parts added for a dramatic purpose.[3] This work of fiction is for entertainment purposes only and is NOT to be treated as a matter of fact or as the ground for theories. However, the publisher and author support the continuation of education and learning. This publication may be included as a subject to study and criticise in the language arts, literature, culture, psychology, or any other related department or faculty.[4] We provide a bibliography at the end of this book for the readers to look further into. If this publication leads the readers to reread the sources, then this literary art publication serves its purpose.[5] The manuscript and cover of this publication are not generated by any artificial intelligence system.[6] No part of this publication may be used to develop and/or train artificial intelligence models, systems, or technology, with no exception for any AI-related uses that fall under the category of fair use or general-purpose AI. No part of this publication that has been made publicly available online may be used in general web scrapping, text and data mining practices, and/or any AI-related transformative uses."[7]

3. The first part is to disclose that the work is an adaptation or adaptive literature. We learnt it from the myth of Medusa. Tattoos of her figure have given empowerment to assault survivors. That one is according to the Roman version of her myth, a retelling by Ovid in *Metamorphoses*. It was an adaptation of the Greek version of her myth. In *Theogony*, Hesiod depicted Medusa in very much different ways.

4. Without having to do the extra paperwork to contact the publisher or me, higher educational institutions or research programmes can utilise my works. Our indie publishing is still a small team to this day; this part will save us some time in giving administrative approvals.

5. This one is to further emphasis point number 4. It is to save them some more time and effort in finding the main sources. Gatekeeping is not what the publisher nor I into. Those academic study paper, research report or journal publication can potentially give us more valuable feedback in the future. They are for others to learn further as well.

6. Readers might think that the sentence is to give author's transparency to the readers, but it is not. This sentence is for the book distribution (and aggregator) platforms to correctly classify the books.

7. The last part is to give the first layer of defence in mining and scrapping. Not that we do not want the percentage of samples to be viewed by potential readers, but we need all part of the publication to remain behind the paywall. It is about the terms of "fair use" (in the US) and "general-purpose" (in the EU).

Regardless of the intended addressees, if the fair warning and disclaimer give the readers of my books better reading experiences, then we shall have much better feedback for us to hear.

4

Editorial Review

Practices for Beginners

There has been a recurring discourse on social media about whether the book reviewing process can be a paid service or should remain a voluntary activity. Are any of you familiar with the following questions?

1. Is it ethical to get a paid review?
2. Is it legal to pay for a book review?

What mostly has not been elaborated is the type of review in the discourse. There are customer (or user) reviews, editorial reviews, and peer reviews.

The customer reviews are also known as user reviews. This topic will be further elaborated in the next two chapters. For now, we will discuss editorial and peer-reviewing processes.

The editorial review is common practice in the publishing industry, research and development (R&D) programmes, and journalism. This chapter hopefully can be beneficial if any of you want to pursue a career in one of those fields.

***

Editorial reviewing in R&D programmes is part of the peer review process.

In the editorial review phase, it is about how the written work clearly communicates the value. The reviewer mostly focuses on how the clarity potentially gives comprehension to different types of users (or readers). Not all of the readers are customers.

The peer review phase focuses on technicalities and applicability. This is when the written work is evaluated as being valid and whether it can be relied on, and most importantly, how the values within can be applicable in operations or the everyday world in general.

Not everyone or random individuals can review those nonfiction books, research reports, or journal publications. The reviewer needs to be either academia in the same or related field of study, licensed or certified practitioners in the field, or industry experts.

It may or may not be ethical to pay for those editorial review and peer review services. The type of institution (or business) and the requirements of professions determine the ethics of the reviewing process.

Every R&D programme has its own standard of structure, list of content, and formatting for the reviews. Even different industry fields or studies have their own standards than others.

By the fact that I am neither an expert in all industries nor in all fields of study on the planet, I shall not give further guidelines on this type of editorial and peer review.

***

Journalists are to conduct their work within the code of ethics in journalism. Imagine Columnist A, who has the qualifications in the field of study around the subject of the book being reviewed. Journalist B had enough experience in that particular industry before working for a media company.

Both when they work in a team may or may not be considered peers or experts to review the book. Their small team may even be considered a review board of its own.

In journalism, the senior or middle editor is the one who does the editorial review of an article manuscript. Then it is an editorial review process of an editorial review article of a book.

These professionals work independently and then get paid by their media company. By that, the book reviewing process becomes paid labour, as in employer-employee compensation.

Can the editorial review article be classified as an indirect paid review? That depends on one's perception.

For print media, the word count heavily depends on the allocated space or block. The type of font and the spacing are standardised by the media company. One time, the column needs to be filled with more words. At some other time, one article needs to be edited to fit the space.

In digital media, the word count requirement may vary. Some companies factor in user interface and user experience throughout the article.

The user interface relates to all the elements being displayed on the online article. The layout of text, images, stickers, and other elements is to retain the readers' viewing time on the article's page.

The user experience is about the readers' engagement with the article being published, i.e., likes, comments, and shares. Eventually, it can lead the readers towards a book being reviewed or push the readers backwards from it.

***

It may become a grey area when a published author provides a paid editorial review service for another author's book.

Even when the category or trope is similar to what the reviewer writes, it needs more careful consideration of whether or not the editorial review can be a paid service. If we compare it with reviewing practices in R&D, the editorial review of a book may or may not be under the peer review umbrella.

One commenter replied to me on social media, saying that it should be the publisher who pays the editorial review service; the author should not. That particular comment alone surely can find us another rabbit hole to dig.

The more days pass, the more self-published books we have to enter the market. Some of the authors might be publishing as individuals. Some others might self-publish under a registered business entity.

Not all of the self-publishing companies plan to become independent publishers to publish others' works. Some of those companies remain to only publish the business founder's works. Here we are, leading ourselves further and deeper in the discourse.

1. On behalf of the author's self-publishing company, will the author be considered as unethical for hiring and compensating editorial reviewers?

2. On behalf of the business entity, is it considered ethical that a self-publishing author pays for the editorial review services?

Putting a signature on a document (or contract) on behalf of the company is different than signing it as an individual. I shall leave you, the readers, with the open-ended questions above.

Whatever the answers will be, eventually they will lead us to further discourse. "How do we separate the artist from the art when the artist is producing and publishing art on behalf of a company?" More about the Creator Economy will be covered later in this book.

***

Each publisher has its own marketing and sales strategies. Obtaining editorial reviews is often one of them.

Choosing which editorial review service provider to hire is sometimes a sales strategy, no longer on the marketing side. It can also help procurement or acquisition divisions of libraries make decisions on which book to carry. Not all libraries receive huge funding.

One provider has a different demographic audience than others. After reading editorial reviews by the service provider they trust, the library might be able to make decisions with more sufficient data. This is when the readers who become editorial reviewers play an important role in the community.

Service providers set their word count requirement for the reviewers. Some set 200 words, 300 words, or 400 words; some others even set a 15-minute video. The requirement increases or decreases in alignment with the providers' track records in the industry.

The rates for services also vary, both from provider to publisher and from provider to reviewers. It can also be because of the number of experts available to review compared to the number of publications in the particular subject or category.

Not all books are being accepted by the service provider. It can be because of the availability of their human capital, the category of the book that does not align with their brand or audience, or simply because the time is too close to the publication date.

The publisher either keeps the editorial reviews as documentation or publishes them on their website. The key points are often printed as a quote on the back cover of the book being published. This is one of the reasons providers commonly set the time limit prior to the publication date.

***

In the hardback journal version, there are spaces for journalers to practise writing editorial reviews. Everyone starts running by taking the first step as a baby, including me. Even one might start walking as a baby, while others start as toddlers.

The editorial review that I do for my colleagues' works is within the process of technical writing issuance for the specific field of work. Even though that is a part of my duty in my main job, I do not (and am not supposed to) provide any editorial review service for written works for other industries.

Please do not compare yourselves to where I am today. Not as an editorial reviewer in my areas of expertise, nor as a published author for the general public. Imposter syndrome is not worth anyone's time.

To end this chapter, I shall leave the judgement for the ethics of conduct to each industry and the legality of operational practices to the governing body of each region. None of the judgements about the said paid services are mine to pass.

THEME
☐ MAJOR

☐ MINOR

☐ UNIVERSAL

PLOT
☐ STRONG
☐ MEDIUM
☐ WEAK

PACE
☐ FAST
☐ MEDIUM
☐ SLOW

CONFLICT
☐ INTERNAL
☐ EXTERNAL:
   CHARACTER VS

WORDCOUNT
TARGET FOR
THIS REVIEW
☐ 100 WORDS
☐ 150 WORDS
☐ 200 WORDS

Image 4.1. Editorial Review Template

5

Reviewing the Advanced Reader Edition

(or Advanced Reader Copy)

Here are some frequently asked questions (FAQs) about Advanced Reader Edition (ARE) that circulate among the book community on social media:

1. What's an ARC? How do I get one?
2. Do we tag the author on social media or not?
3. If it's 3-star or lower, when do I post the review? Do I post it on the publishing date or wait a few weeks later?
4. What if life gets busier? Should I tell the author that I'll be late posting a review?

From what we have been watching or reading on social media, there are a lot more essentials about this topic. To this date, my publisher and I keep holding back from giving away AREs.

The first reason is that we still have a small team as an independent publisher. We are travellers who do not have the space yet to add more tasks to our schedules. The second reason is that we want to give the final products instead of the pre-publication edition.

We call the receivers ARE reviewers; at least in our team, we do not refer to you as ARC readers. The term "Advanced Reader

Copy Readers" does not sound right, does it? Besides, it might not put the proper mindset about it.

Some witches might say that words are spells. That might be true, because wordsmiths spell the words that we write, do we not? Please do not mind my punning word puzzle; that is not the point here.

By using the term "ARC reader", the goal might only be for the receiver to read the book. What authors and publishers aim for is for the receivers to read and review the book. We might as well save some time and effort by clarifying it from the start.

The term AREs might also sound unfamiliar to your ears. At least, in our small team, we call the pre-publication edition AREs, as in the Greek god Ares. It sounds more theatrical in our ears.

Mind you, this very author has been trying so hard to make this user guide sound a bit more serious for readers to take me seriously. But so far, the author has not found any success in achieving the goal.

Working for my main job, looking and acting stoic are necessary most times. So when I am not doing my main job, there is a tendency to vent out humour, puns, and banter; only the sarcasm and saltiness miss the memo.

Yes, of course, working in a male-dominated field has its own challenges. Writing fiction works always feels like having outbursts. I do not feel like working when working on fiction projects; the author is having a me time in the playground.

Even while working on this user guide project, I feel like talking to acquaintances. Have you not realised how many teas have been spilt in this book so far? Many more to come until the end of this book. The publishing team surely will add more seasoning in the last four chapters.

***

In some regions, the pre-publication edition needs a different ISBN (or so-called dummy ISBN) than the one that is going to be published for the market. Those two are to differentiate the SKU so that the AREs will not be resold or redistributed to others.

This is what we think receivers need to ask before enrolling in the ARE reviewing programme: "Is this copy a final product or a pre-publication edition?"

There is a probability that authors or publishers do not disclose the difference between the two. One of the reasons is to avoid the risk of piracy. Regardless, the question might help receivers to review based on the data provided by the time the AREs are distributed.

It is not about lowering the standard of the rating system that the readers hold. It is hopefully for the reviewers to fully understand that the pre-publication edition being given is not the final product.

Can the version uphold the bar to the same height as the final one in the rating systems? That depends on one's perception and might be different from one reviewer to another.

There are two possible cases here. If the AREs are the pre-publication edition, the ARE reviews might not fall into the customer review category. It is more likely to be part of the marketing strategies.

In this first case, ARE reviewers become the agents to help publishers sell the book. The reviewers might need to find specific factors while reading it. Here are some of the things that might need highlighting:

1. Who will be the ideal reader for the book? Their interest, their trope preference, the background, and anything related to the demographic or even socioeconomic factors.

2. Why should anyone read the book regardless of the price point? At the ARE phase, the price might not be announced yet. It is better to assume that it would be priced sky high than the middle price point. The publisher or author might need the book to be perceived as "worth the money" by potential readers.

***

If the AREs are the final product, there is a high chance that the publisher will see the ARE reviews as customer reviews. For this case, the further explanations will be in the next chapter.

☆☆☆☆☆

PLOT
☐ STRONG
☐ MEDIUM
☐ WEAK

PACE
☐ FAST
☐ MEDIUM
☐ SLOW

PLOT
☐ STRONG
☐ MEDIUM
☐ WEAK

PACE
☐ FAST
☐ MEDIUM
☐ SLOW

☆☆☆☆☆

Image 5.1. ARE Review Template

6

Customer Review

(or User Review)

There are these being repeatedly found on social media:

1. Authors should take readers' feedback into consideration.
2. Reviews are for the readers, not for the authors! It's a readers' space.

As we can see, the two statements seem to contradict each other. Most times, I read the two sides of the book community with giggles.

The unspoken words that cross my mind usually are, "Do you want us to read your reviews or not? You got me confused." And now the unspoken has been spoken.

***

There have been other authors besides me with similar confusion about whether or not the readers want us to write in the first place. Over the internet, we find so many "Authors Do and Don't" or "Authors Can & Cannot" that come from, mostly, not published authors.

At one time, I replied to one author's comment on another author's post with something like, "... or they are aspiring authors, but... haven't got to the 'crying to sleep at night when publishing the book' part yet."

That phase in book publication is wild. It is a business, but we remain humankind who can feel our feelings. There are so many emotions involved in creating our literary arts.

Not every process in the back office is (or should be) posted online. There are multiple phases of editing in book publication. If you did not know, now you do. Authorship is a business in the publishing industry; some even refer to it as authorpreneurship.

In my main job, most times I say, "Yooo... I ain't spilling tea, fam! The thingy is confidential." Of course, it is the polished version with explicit language expressions being scratched out. Mind you, confidentiality is much higher than signed NDAs.

Authorpreneurship is a mindset and work ethic in the business of publishing copyrighted works. Almost every business has its own "business secret" to keep. That is one of the functions of NDAs.

Not everyone is used to working in the dark. None of what I write in this user guide can go out to see the daylight unless the publisher approves it for publication. There is plenty of information in this user guide that has not been talked about on social media.

If this publication can give any aspiring author a glimpse through the veil towards our back office during publication, then this book serves its purpose to guide others.

The aspirant will pierce the veil when one starts writing book number one. Once one aspirant walks through the veil, then things we cover in this user guide will resonate.

In case loneliness knocks on your door, reread this book; you are not alone in the dark, because we are in this together, building our legacies. Those who say or tell us the "Authors Do and Don't" or "Authors Can & Cannot" might not realise it, but our literary arts are our legacies, not theirs.

***

It is about time to return to this statement: "Authors should take readers' feedback into consideration."

Reflecting on the statement above, here is a mirror for anyone who needs it: "Are you an editorial reviewer or a peer to review the written work?"

Once the beta reading phase has passed, the editing processes are already in the past. Some readers might not realise it. There will be no going back to the editing phases and using the same ISBN at the same time.

Here is another mirror in case anyone needs an extra: "Are you a professional editor? If yes, have we ever given any compensation for your editing service?"

If the answer to the questions in this section is a hard "no", then we shall view your feedback as customer (or user) reviews for the future edition of the book. That will be another project to undergo with new budget planning.

Personally, I would prefer to call it "customer review" rather than "user review". One day, hopefully, you are going to be accustomed to my writings. The word 'consumer' is different from 'customer' in business.

As for the statement, "Reviews are for the readers, not for the authors! It's a readers' space" it is going to be an inevitable grey area for self-published authors. Businesses need to be evaluated periodically.

The customer reviews become the customer feedback for the business. When an author self-publishes the book, the author is indeed the business. The customer review space then merges to be the self-publisher's space at the same time.

There are authors who are not keen on reading those customer reviews. We can hire staff to do the evaluation on behalf of the business. Evaluation is to forecast the future of the operations.

***

We have sent countless of them to bookish creators. We keep pushing promotional content for my contemporary romance on social media. And yet, my contemporary works that had been planned will be postponed.

I shall be limited to one contemporary publication annually. One work being published in a year is enough reason for me to be grateful for.

This very author is glad that the historical novels will still go for publication as scheduled. I do not have any other choice than being glad; 'Rada' literally means 'glad'. You might ask the reasons for the postponement by now.

It is because of one thing: the monthly compensation reports from all distribution platforms. From the business perspective, the reports are the feedback. We have been pushing the contemporary works regularly, but it has been the historical romance that converts.

It took us almost a year to revise my debut novel for the second edition. While undergoing the revision, only a few times have I posted anything about my historical romance novels. Without being pushed on social media, my historical romance keeps bringing compensation in.

Those conversions keep on coming, mostly from outside of the US. It makes me wonder whether or not VPN pseudonymity really works.

The social media analytics are mostly in line with the pseudonymous location. When we compare them to the compensation reports, they seem to be two different magnetic poles. Regardless, we are grateful for each conversion made on whatever part of planet Earth.

I might be as clueless as you are; I do not know how it happened that way. If you are an (aspiring) author or bookish content creator, please stop being hard on yourselves about social media.

***

Surprisingly, the conversions come more regularly since we raised the ebook price. Now there is another discourse about ebook prices.

We were once lost in a rabbit hole after revising a book. My technical writing works were mostly not published to the public for them to need any ISBN.

The publisher's team members have experience in publications and media companies, but not in the US. Each region has its own laws and regulations.

In some parts of the world, there have been ISBN shortages. That is hypothetically a downside of when government bodies give them away for free. Many of the books in where we came from got delayed, if not cancelled, because of it. My publisher and I are people from those regions.

It took us quite some time to research whether we need a different ISBN for the digital version of the revised edition. We actually got plenty of help from the people in the technology and gaming industries.

Then we learnt that it is similar to what we refer to as "version control" systems in technical writing. Since then, we have added "Publisher's Note" in the front matter for every content update.

It is licensing to access the content. For anyone who has ever paid for or been given access to the digital version of my books, sync your devices to get the latest version update.

Access to the latest version of content is what licensing payors have that print copy buyers do not. Yes, I am fully aware when writing the words 'payors' and 'buyers'. The two pay for two different things.

Please consider revising the customer review once anyone finishes reading the updated version of an ebook, that is, if the book reviewing platform allows. It will help us, authors and publishers.

***

We have been receiving messages offering paid "verified purchase" reviews. My publisher and I have to say no to offers from those accounts.

To write customer reviews, you have the choice whether to write them for the publisher and author or for the potential readers. Choosing the addressees is not about honest or dishonest reviews, but about choosing your writing style.

When reviewing for the publisher and author, readers will write to provide feedback for future revisions. It can be regarding the story itself, the authorship, or the price point.

Choosing fellow readers as your addressee provides valuable insight for the ideal audience. Probably, it will be more practical if you write customer reviews with the mindset of a matchmaker than a so-called marketing agent.

With the matchmaking mindset, there is a possibility for you to simultaneously build your community as content creators. It is not only matching books to their ideal readers, but also matching your social media platform to your ideal audience—the ones who have similar reading preferences to you.

As for bookish content creators, further explanation about content creation will be in the next four chapters. The contributor for the topic is none other than the publisher of this user guide.

The team is the one who has more experience in the media and information industry—in print, digital, video, and audio formats. The idea of me explaining the matter by myself does not seem right to me.

This is the end of my portion for the user guide. We shall meet again through my other written works. The publisher will take it from here.

7

For Bookish Creators

by the Publisher

Register the business as soon as possible!
We have learnt our lessons... the hard way.

***

We have always wanted to deliver these valuable lessons for a while but never had any project to be a vehicle for it. Finally, there is this book. The value aligns and might be relevant to its readers.

Acquaintances should not have been lost in the process. Energy could have been preserved. Time could have been kept. Money could have been saved. By a lot!

Please exercise caution with individuals who use terms like collab, internship, and even co-author. Be mindful that they will come to you one day, and everyone should be prepared to make inconvenient decisions.

Consider registering the content creation business as soon as you see any collaboration or agreement coming. Even if it will be a company of one, consider separating yourself from the business.

Here we are putting aside our perspective as an independent book publisher. Let us step back into the content creator's perspective for the sake of completing this project.

***

We started by making educational content on social media almost a decade ago. It was 2016, to be exact, but only in 2021 did we incorporate the business.

Within those gap years, there were hundreds of videos made with thousands of minutes, if not millions, of recordings. Yes, we added seasoning to the previous sentence. There was tons of paperwork for the transfer of rights for those videos.

Imagine two long-form videos per week only for one channel. No, we never have only one channel. One niche for each channel. Each channel has its target audience.

Why YouTube and not other platforms? Because our team is in the marathon-mind game. That is the simple answer, as we need to make it less complicated for now.

The schedules of our main jobs limit us from constantly chasing our tail on social media. It is the main factor when choosing the main social media platform to deliver our content. Your circumstances might be different from ours, as each content is different.

We took a break for almost two years to focus on publishing books. Our audience might not realise it has been that long because we schedule-posted our content two to three months before we laid low.

In fact, by the time this book is published, we have not returned to our regular posting schedule yet. During that long break, even until now, those published videos keep on converting. Videos from years ago are still being watched as we write this.

Participants keep on enrolling in our online courses to this day; even compensations from our books keep on coming. Our hypotheses have been given a conclusion by those numbers in the reports.

We gave up chasing vanity metrics years ago, as we consider it a plan for the sprint. Virality, views, watch time, subscriber count, and follower count no longer matter in our company.

The values we deliver through our content need to endure the test of time, at least for a few years ahead. This book is one of them; hopefully, the values written in here will endure.

There are still many projects queuing to be published in a year or two ahead. For each book we publish, we call it a "project", not a "book manuscript". Each time we work on a manuscript for publication, it is the development of a project. At least for our team, it is, as in a business.

***

Regardless of the language or the format, content is content. There is an audience for each niche, format, and type of content.

Content can be in the form of video, photographs, audio, or even words on a website or book. Let's not forget that the author R.L. Zareva (or Rada Lyubomirova) can be considered a content creator, only in the written form.

Our cofounders are people from the East who have been constantly travelling. Those journeys we walked have opened many opportunities. The further we go away from where we came from, the more doors are opening for us. Only in 2022 did we start publishing our content in English.

If video is where you perform best, then make it and click (or tap) publish. It all started by making content in our cofounders' native language. If your content performs best in your native language, then make a conversation in the spoken language.

We just learnt around last year that localisation has its own advantages. Not everything needs to be written or spoken in English, as not everyone speaks English.

The conversations build a connection with the audience because there is something in common between the creator and the community. The relationship with the audience is retained because the value is relevant to them.

Fast forward to today; we try to reach the people in the far and beyond. Never have we imagined that our books would reach places that none of our team members have even visited yet. This is how fascinated our team is by the internet capability.

***

Every creator has a different area of strength. If copywriting is your strongest one, then fill in the photo caption with it.

Write those book reviews on the main bookish platform of your preference, then distribute them on different platforms. Utilise the material that you already have.

We are aware that each content creator is different and has different goals. Each bookish creator is also different from one another. Some of the bookish creators do it for the hobby; others might be doing it to simply be able to put their hands on the print books.

There are many different reasons for readers not to be able to obtain print books. We, people from the East, understand that completely. Shipping and cargo have always been a huge cost. On top of that, customs clearance takes time for the book to arrive. These factors remain to this day.

Even some of the books we have read in the past needed to be cleared by the intelligence agencies in the said region. Those agencies' stamps of approval on the first page of the books definitely could not be unseen.

We grew up with those hardships only to read books. Nevertheless, those hardships have given us a sense of gratitude. If we had never experienced any of them in our upbringing, we would not have a tale to tell through this user guide.

The next two chapters will be long ones. Brace for impact! Brace. Brace. Brace.

8

Creating Content Plans

by the Publisher

Some of you, readers, might already be familiar with the phrase "niche down".

Remember that one social media page can always pivot from one niche to another anytime necessary. We have rebranded our platforms many times, probably more times than our audience even realised.

We did mention in the previous chapter, "One niche for each channel." It is best for you to avoid comparing yourselves with our team.

We can say it that way after years of making content. Please remember that every creator starts with zero followers. For anyone new to creating content, simply start with one page on one platform and then grow it.

***

The first step is listing the book category or trope that you are keen on reading. Write it down in the journal so you can visualise it. Remember, at this step, everything is about anything that you already have within you and in your surroundings.

Presumably, you already have a sense of self-awareness to tell whether you are an informative or entertaining person. The type of content follows the kind of person you are.

One informative creator might be better at making educational types of content. If the creator's personality is cheerful and humorous in real life, it might be practical for the creator to make entertaining content.

In the future, the two will possibly be merged, so the creator can be influential, even enlightening, to others. As of now, make a list in the journal of what you already have in your space that you like and can bring value to others.

***

The term "creator economy" has been around for almost three decades. It was Paul Saffo of Stanford University who first mentioned the term around 1997. On YouTube, the term switched from "user" to "creator" around 2011.

Has it not reached the book community yet? If it had not, well, now it has. Step two is setting up the business and registering the company. It is easy to think, "Is it not too early?"

This is not about getting ready to charge publishers or authors early in your content creation journey. This step is about getting ready to open the door for any time opportunity that comes. Think about putting a "Welcome" doormat on your patio.

Before we go further into the business side of content creation, let us ask. Have you ever wondered any of these:

1. I only ever get eARC so far. How do I get physical ones?
2. How can anyone get the PR packages? Do I have to have a huge following on social media?

There is one important question to ask the sender before anyone gives the mailing address: *"Am I required to make any content about the things I am about to receive?"*

In some regions, the answer to the question may (or may not) be considered a handshake of an agreement. If the answer is yes, it may (or may not) be considered a non-monetary income, depending on your tax residency.

If the answer is no, there is a chance that the publisher or author plans to deduct them as business gifts, depending on where their business tax registration is.

Creators need to ask a Certified Public Accountant (CPA) or a taxation lawyer about this matter. It is about **who** is going to report **what** in **which** tax reporting form.

You will not know unless the other party discloses it; that is an internal matter of how one practises the business. Not in every region is everyone required to disclose anything, either.

***

Before continuing to the income part, we need to understand the cost of creating content.

Since this book is niched down for content creators who love to read, of course, your content is most likely about books. While Rada Lyubomirova prefers to call it "customer review" instead of "user review". We, the publisher, prefer the opposite.

Social media creators (or influencers) have started making user-generated content (UGC). The term might be more common in the lifestyle influencer community than in the book community. Within the last few years, the UGC business has grown in popularity.

Some of the creators include the products or services they receive through the partnership or collaboration. That way, the cost can be reduced. Each partnership is different; creators can either be contractors or exclusive (or non-exclusive) brand ambassadors.

You, as bookish content creators, might not have received any physical ARE or promotional package yet. This is not to dishearten any of you. Because of this, there is a budget to plan.

Anyone can start by reviewing the ones available in the house and maximising the surrounding environment. Some prefer to build their home studios, while others prefer to save the budget and use free natural light.

Here is when the business registration comes into play. Ask the public accountant who is certified or the lawyer who practises in taxation in your tax residency.

Ask either of them about the kind of items that are allowed to be written off as tax deductibles and what the limit is for each item. Each taxation agency in each region has its own tax-deductible list with various limitations on the amount.

Ask either of them specifically about your bookish content creation business. Ask if books are allowed to be included as deductibles in tax reporting when doing your business. Ask about how much is within the limits. Ask. Ask. Ask... in detail.

This is the end of step three. We shall leave you with the matter here, since we are neither certified nor given any licence to practise in taxation in any region.

***

The main reason we prefer to refer to it as 'user reviews' is simply because the user already has the material within reach. We know this because we have been making UGC or CGC over the years.

Step four is about maximising what we have. From reading books that are already sitting on your shelves or borrowed from the libraries, you write user reviews and post them to bookish platforms. As long as you write the reviews by yourself, they can be converted into UGC.

If the social media platform allows long captions (or descriptions), surely the easiest way is to turn the reviews into copywriting. They can be used for the photo captions.

For creators who are comfortable with talking in front of the camera, remember that you already have archives. The user reviews can be transformed into video scripts.

It may sound hard to read the scripts at first, but they do not necessarily need to be spoken out as news anchors read their teleprompter. Even now, our team still uses bullet points in the notebook while recording.

We first published this book as a guided journal along with the digital version. The paperback print book will follow about six months later than the ebook. There are reasons for it.

One of them is for you to write the review with a pen on paper. Remember when we mentioned writing the reviews by yourself? So when it is time for you to convert it into video scripts, you will only recall prior knowledge about the book.

It is intentional to recall the moment you read the book, the moment you write the review on paper, the moment you reread it prior to posting, and when typing the review online. The information is already vaulted in your head.

There is no need to be stressed for recording day, but it is important to be prepared. Here is what has been happening in our team. What is written as bullet points can expand during the recording day. Things that spontaneously cross our minds on the spot surely add details our bullet points might miss.

What happens in the surroundings during the recording day can easily add something to our recordings. Roll with it. No matter how hilarious your expression looks, keep the camera rolling. No one can guarantee whether the recorded events will be recurring.

Time flies easily and fast on recording day. DSLRs are limited to 29 minutes or so for each recording. You might not know how many times our cameras automatically stop recording. Here we tell you: countless times.

Whether those spontaneous and unpredictable events will be needed in the final video or not, it is nothing to think about for now. For our team, at least, we would prefer to have extra recordings rather than fewer.

On a batch-recording day, we usually can get 6–8 raw footages. Those can be divided into up to two months of weekly content for different channels. The more years our team makes videos, the more we need to cut our raw footage into shorter videos.

Time is the asset and currency at the same time here. Those extra recordings are assets that can buy us some time in the algorithm when we need extra days (or weeks) off.

It depends on the main social media platform of your preference. Some social media may need a few days to breathe in between postings; others may need multiple posts on a daily basis to retain the performance.

***

Step five is projecting the income streams. The previous sentence includes a plural form. When starting out, start with one; the rest will follow.

The most accessible income source when we were starting out was affiliate programmes. When you scan the QR code we provide in this book, you will see plenty of affiliate links being listed. Still to this day, they keep generating income for our team.

Bookish creators do not need to have connections to any publisher or author to be affiliates. From the publisher's perspective, this is a better way than charging self-published debut authors for social media shoutouts.

There are many affiliate programme marketplaces available online. Some of them even have instant approval, disregarding your vanity metrics.

Another source of income is the Creator Fund. Different social media platforms have different requirements for their programmes. One thing to remember is that we want loyal audiences, not ones who click out of our video to visit the advertiser's website.

Content creators who have built a fan base might flourish with the fund programme. Other creators flourish from conversions towards the businesses outside of the fund.

9

Social Media Rate Card

by the Publisher

Some content has educational elements; others have promotional elements. This very user guide or guided journal is a merge between the two.

The digital version gets published first because the manuscript is filled with SEO (Search Engine Optimization). It feels unnatural to spell the last word of the previous sentence with the letter -z-.

For the sake of the metadata, we spelt it "optimization" instead of "optimisation". Can you see that the past tense form of the word "spell" in the previous sentence was spelt "spelt", not "spelled"?

"Why does it matter?" We have also seen user reviews mentioning typos or misspellings. We are aware that not everyone is aware that not every author writes with US spelling.

We are sometimes unaware of our device settings changing from English (UK) to English (US) or vice versa. Our team, too, often forgets to change it back.

"How does this matter again?" We have learnt it from making paid content in the past. The video description is where we fill in the metadata. The misspellings are regarding the written words. There is something that is worse than misspellings for content that has audio in it.

Vocal fry at the end of the sentence is potentially being read as "inaudible". The social media platform might transcribe them as unreadable in automatic CC. That way, it may impact how the algorithm pushes the content you post.

If anyone asks about pieces of equipment to invest in, we spontaneously answer "sound equipment". But those will not matter if the creator speaks unclearly. No equipment may be able to help fix it.

Not until quarter four of 2016 did we upload our first video. At the beginning of that year, we enrolled in voice trainings with radio announcers. We practised it almost every day before making any content.

It is not about the accent or dialect of the content creator. It is about the clarity of spoken words, especially when shouting out book titles and the author's name.

Since we are discussing clear communication, we might as well add this info. Presumably, R.L. Zareva is easy enough for readers to pronounce. It is not wrong if creators address the author with the pen name. Choose whichever is practical to build your audience.

/ Rā.da.Lu.bŏ.mī.ro.va / is the phonetic symbol of Рада Любомирова. For the books written by her, we transliterate the name as "Rada Lyubomirova".

"You can choose either one," she said. "It's just a name," she said. Here, you have the author's permission being relayed.

***

We have only mentioned shoutouts so far. Shall we continue to build a rate card (or quotation) for when you offer services? No, no, not so fast! It would be helpful to set up the boundaries first.

We start with the least amount of fee to the potential highest. Creator A can be featured on Creator B's page in exchange for Creator B being featured on Creator A's page. The topic can be the same or different. Content-Content Collaboration might be the easiest form of all.

What we refer to as a "mention" or "shoutout" is actually putting the brand's social media handle in the description (or caption) or tagging the brand in our post. In some deals, it can also include pronouncing the brand in a post, but the video itself is actually about some other topic.

The lengthened version of the shoutout is "Sponsored Post". The ad lib is commonly inserted in the middle of a video that has a longer duration. Some contracts even state the exact minute and duration to place it.

Dedicated posts are usually the longest to produce. An unboxing video can be considered the shorter version of it. Most times, dedicated posts involve an A-roll explainer, B-roll footage, and a thorough look at the product being highlighted.

Creators in some regions (or countries) are required to add disclosure for the paid collaboration or sponsorship. If we are to give an unbiased review of the product or service, we usually wait for a duration of time. And then we make another review video.

The follow-up video is usually excluded from the paid contract, but each contract is different. It can be a user review of a book that is converted into a UGC video. One thing can lead to another and lead further in the future. We commonly call it Creator-Generated Content (CGC).

The gifted partnership is what commonly builds CGC. Gift-Content Collaboration has many names that are sometimes confusing for new content creators. There is no money involved in this type. The bookish creator will receive a book in exchange for content to feature it on the creator's page.

This type of collaboration relies heavily on which region you are in. Each region has different views when discerning whether the gifted product or service itself is non-monetary compensation.

The value of the book is to be reported in the creator's tax reports if you are in the region that considers it a non-monetary compensation. As mentioned in the previous chapter, it is important to ask about the requirements prior to signing a deal.

These are some of the terms for the same type of collaboration: gifted collaboration, influencer gifting collaboration, in-kind partnership, etc.

The next one is paid collaboration, which is when a bookish creator receives a book from an author or publisher and gets paid for making content featuring the book.

In one region, the book is considered a non-monetary compensation on top of the amount of money being paid. In other regions, the book is excluded from the tax report. Once again, it is important to be well-informed before agreeing to any collaboration.

If the author or publisher does business in a different country than the creator, everything needs to be cleared prior to the shipment. Not only for tax reporting purposes, but also for customs clearance if the governing body where the receiver resides enforces tariffs.

The PR Box (or Package) is commonly a risk of doing business as an author or a publisher. In some regions, it is a tax-deductible item. The downside of it is that there is no agreement or guarantee that the content creator will ever make any content featuring the book or the author.

Spokesperson or brand ambassador deals involve more detail to pay attention to. Content that the creator made is to be posted on the brand's page. The typical paperwork is release consent, commercial use licence, and broadcast licence.

For administrative purposes, the creators' agency or talent management could be helpful. Not every creator needs to sign up with any agency. It depends on your needs at the stage of your content creation.

***

Finally, we come to the part of building a rate card (or quotation) for the content creator services. In order to make one, each creator needs to have the valuations of all platforms that the creator utilises.

From short to long duration. Content with ratios from horizontal to square, and to vertical. The question below comes from a team that has been producing and managing content for almost a decade on multiple platforms. With humility, we humbly ask this question of the bookish content creators who read this book:

> *"After receiving your social media valuations, are you certain to charge any fee to self-published authors who have invested their time and hundreds, if not thousands, of dollars out of their pocket when publishing their books, especially debut authors?"*

Since the first day of planning this project, we have been aware of the possibility of the readers being aspiring authors. Please be considerate when planning the way to monetise your content; one day, one of you might be walking in our shoes.

We have heard many bookish content creators say, "Supporting indie authors." Once someone offers any service to publishers or authors, the content creator may (or may not) become an open-for-hire contractor. The publisher or author is the one who hires.

It depends on what is considered a handshake of agreement in which region; either being an ARE reviewer or a street team member, the content creator might be considered to be receiving non-monetary compensation.

This part is not about our team trying to humble-brag about our experience. Over the years, we have learnt how to calculate social media accounts, either automatically or manually. From the 24-hour temporary post to the permanent one, all have different valuations.

Even the permanent posts have a shelf life of performance in the algorithm. Our platforms' valuations vary from a couple to hundreds of US dollars per post. Please consider other ways to monetise your social media content rather than charging authors or self-publishers.

For digital version readers, we add the list of providers for social media valuation that you can look up. If anyone is certain of offering services to publishers or authors, make the quotation as clear as possible before ever signing anything.

Below are items commonly included in a quotation for 1 (one) type of service. If one offers more than one service, then each service needs to be broken down.

1. Content format: text, photo, or video.

2. Ratio for non-text content: 16:9, 1:1, or 9:16.

3. Copywriting for non-text content: included or excluded.

4. Script for video content: included or excluded.

5. Social media platform: _____ *(specify)*

6. Shelf life: temporary *(24-hour, 1-week, or _____)* or permanent.

7. The type of influencer marketing: shoutout, sponsored post, dedicated post, or spokesperson.

8. The type of collaboration: content-content, gift-content, or

9. Fee for the service: $_____

Cost Estimation

TO PRODUCE CONTENT

MAXIMUM BUDGET: QUARTER/YEAR:

SOCIAL MEDIA PLATFORMS: CONTENT QTY

☐

☐ MAIN   ☐ DISTRIBUTION   ☐ DAILY   ☐ WEEKLY

☐

☐ MAIN   ☐ DISTRIBUTION   ☐ DAILY   ☐ WEEKLY

☐

☐ MAIN   ☐ DISTRIBUTION   ☐ DAILY   ☐ WEEKLY

BUDGET:
☐ BOOK BUYING
☐ EBOOK PLATFORM MEMBERSHIP
☐ AUDIOBOOK PLATFORM MEMBERSHIP
☐ EQUIPMENT
☐ TOOLS
☐ OTHER BOOKISH MERCHANDISE

Image 9.1. Cost Estimation

PROJECTION

GOAL: % OF THE BUDGET   QUARTER/YEAR:

INCOME SOURCES: CONVERSION TARGET

☐

☐ ACTIVE   ☐ PASSIVE   ☐ MONTHLY ☐ WEEKLY

☐

☐ ACTIVE   ☐ PASSIVE   ☐ MONTHLY ☐ WEEKLY

☐

☐ ACTIVE   ☐ PASSIVE   ☐ MONTHLY ☐ WEEKLY

GOALS:
☐ AFFILIATE MARKETING
☐ MERCHANDISE SALES
☐ DIGITAL PRODUCTS
☐ CREATOR FUND
☐ SPONSORSHIP
☐ BRAND DEAL

Image 9.2. Income Projection

10

Important Notes

from the Author and Publisher

Some feedback said that within the first few pages, they thought that it was not the book for them. That was all right. Rada Lyubomirova does not usually splay everything out in the first quarter of the book.

From a couple of chapters in the beginning, one might assume that her book is about X. Most likely the message within is not; most likely the layers of stories are built about Y halfway through, if not about Z.

Some bookish creators might say that readers of Dostoyevsky, Tolstoy, Akhmatova, Chekov, Turgenev, Bugakov, Lermontov, Gogol, Gorky, Pushkin, Zamyatin, Goncharov, Solzhenitsyn, Karamzin, Solokhov, Ostrovsky, Nobokov, Zoshchenko, or many more are on the "other side" of the bookish community.

The works mentioned earlier might be considered different types of readings for some. In some regions on earth, those are mandatory readings in the school curriculum.

Authors who have read those books mentioned above during their teenage years or young adulthood possibly write their works differently from those who did not. Rada happens to be one of them.

As many have been deceived by Rada Lyubomirova's fiction works, the reader of this book might have been deceived, too. As she mentioned in the beginning of this book, R.L. Zareva's intention was to write a user guide. That was hers, but not the publisher's.

As you might notice, we apply her style of plot twisting in this user guide. If you, as readers, find any value through this user guide or guided journal, that will be beyond our expectations.

From the publisher's standpoint, this user guide is simply a marketing tool to promote her other works. At this point, either you have already seen Rada's portfolio of work in the front matter, or worse, the readers have gone into the rabbit hole by utilising the QR code.

The potential conversion is either towards Rada Lyubomirova's book collection, other authors' books we publish, or the affiliate links listed on the landing page. Either way, you will support our team.

Vanity metrics sound wonderful, but conversion rate matters more for us. Here is what you, as content creators, need to determine: "Where are you leading your audience? What conversion are you generating income from?"

Here is another plot twist: this book is not the only marketing tool. The number of her contemporary novellas that we gave away compared to her historical fiction novels is similar to the high level of the sky compared to the depth of the ocean.

None of the novellas written by Rada Lyubomirova had ever been planned to be a product. They have always been marketing tools for the products—the historical fiction novels.

As for now, readers in the US can get licences to the digital version of the books for free by scanning or tapping the QR code. We provide you with redemption links to access them. If time allows, we will appreciate your feedback.

***

Rada Lyubomirova and all of this publisher's cofounders are, in fact, women who work in male-dominated fields.

From working amongst men, we keep learning about strategising and building alternative plans. The way we develop our projects and how the author tells the story might feel different for some.

Through publishing our books, we have been building bridges from our working environments to your hands. Since day one of us working on Rada's debut novel, we have realised that not every woman has a chance (or is willing) to work in any male-dominated field.

As women in our workforces, we consider it a privilege to have our thought processes challenged. The challenges and competitions are different from those in gender-balanced industries, let alone in female-dominated ones. Plenty of those that we observe and listen to mostly remain unspoken.

The lessons and messages deserve to be relayed. We are to give you a glimpse of our working environments. You might have noticed the covers of Rada's novellas show the MMCs' occupation or activity.

Travelling is a part of our main jobs. The high mobility lifestyle of ours also toughens us up. Many surprising factors on the road teach us many lessons.

Creating content on the internet polishes our level of patience. Both creating content and publishing books require hard work in the here and now.

Regardless, we consider ourselves quite relaxed with the compensations from our books or other digital products for now. Throughout the entirety of this project, we might seem to take everything lightly, even being grateful for every single thing.

Not that we do not take anything seriously, but more that we laugh at life itself many times. Besides, laughter is contagious. From our upbringing being filled with challenges and restrictions to taking our chances in foreign lands, even simple things give us a chance to be thankful.

We bet on ourselves. Never have we ever imagined publishing anything in a foreign land. None of our team members is a native English speaker. Here is the final plot twist in this book: The books we publish are for the future.

We are grateful if they can provide value for others and bring in monetary results for our team in the present time. Our team members are in the marathon mind game, never in a sprint.

The projects that we have been working on are what we consider our retirement funds; as for now, we have our main jobs. For when we pass, all the projects will become our legacies to the future generation of readers and audience.

We hope, once again, the values within our publications are going to stand the test of time to constantly be relevant, including this very book.

Thank you for reading our works. It is time for us to hand over the torch to you, readers.

About R.L. Zareva

Pen Name: Rada Lyubomirova

The first transparency the author is willing to make is that the author is, in fact, a woman.

In the place the author came from, the only gender identity one is allowed to pronounce is the assignment at birth, with heterosexual relationships being the only permitted preference.

She has reached the age of majority to write her adult fiction works. Her works are to be restricted to being read by minors. They are not suitable for readers with sensitivity to certain subjects and/or language expressions.

The second transparency is that she is a descendant of multiple ethnic groups and races. She lives in a household unit in which more ethnic groups and races are being added into the mix.

The author is not willing to break down everything in the mix merely for the sake of the author's transparency. The readers' demand for it has been heard many times on social media; the demand to unmask was neither worth jeopardising authors' safety nor compromising loved ones' well-being.

We appreciate everyone's understanding regarding the matter. Nevertheless, we are to prevent anyone from pretending to be either Rada Lyubomirova or R.L. Zareva over the internet. Since the author will retain her incognita for the future, it is essential to include the author's profile on our website.

About the Publisher

Besides publishing fiction and nonfiction books, Compendia Publishing creates content for social media and online courses.

Scan or tap the QR code above to see our portfolio of works.

***

Thank you for purchasing the original copy of this book. Your feedback will help both the publisher and author with our future works.